THE VIETNAM WAR

JOHN DEVANEY

THE

VIETNAM
WAR

FRANKLIN WATTS

New York ★ Chicago ★ London ★ Toronto ★ Sydney
A First Book

Frontispiece: A Vietnamese woman shrieks in anguish
as she cradles her dead child, a victim of a war that
killed more than 1.5 million people.

Maps by William J. Clipson

Cover photograph copyright © AP/Wide World Photos

Photographs copyright © : Veterans of Foreign Wars: chapter openers;
James H. Pickerell: pp. 2, 29, 32 bottom, 37 top, 41; Woodfin Camp &
Associates: pp. 11, 37 bottom; The John F. Kennedy Library: p. 19;
UPI/Bettmann Newsphotos; pp. 21 top, 32 top, 49; Edward C. Britton,
Sacramento, CA: 21 bottom, 25, 30 top, 35; Tom Myers, Sacramento, CA:
p. 45 bottom; Archive Photos, NY: pp. 22, 44 top; AP/Wide World Photos:
pp. 24, 30 bottom, 43, 44 bottom, 45 top, 52; Gamma-Liaison/Francolon:
p. 53; ProFiles West/Frank Staub: p. 54.

Library of Congress Cataloging-in-Publication Data

Devaney, John.
The Vietnam war / by John Devaney.
p.   cm. — (First book)
Includes index.
Summary: Unveils the horror and the politics of this controversial
war, from the French withdrawal after the Battle of Dien Bien Phu to
the fall of Saigon in 1975.
ISBN 0-531-20046-9
1. Vietnamese Conflict, 1961-1975 — Juvenile literature.
[1. Vietnamese Conflict, 1961-1975.]   I. Title.   II. Series.
DS557.7.D48   1992
959.704'3 — dc20   91-14755 CIP AC

CONTENTS

ONE

DIEN BIEN PHU

THE ENEMY GUNS rained down bombs on the French soldiers. Orange balls of fire and clouds of smoke blinded and choked the soldiers as the bombs blew up around them. Hunks of metal tore into bodies, slicing men in half. Dead men filled the trenches and littered the ground. The wounded, bleeding and moaning, were dragged into trenches to die.

Major Bruno Bigeard, a French paratrooper, peered over the edge of his muddy trench. With his binoculars he could see the enemy guns belch red flame. Then the enemy pulled the cannons into caves high in the mountains. The French guns could not fire back at the hidden guns whose shells were slowly wiping them out.

A few months ago, Bigeard had parachuted into this valley called Dien Bien Phu with more than a thousand paratroopers. Today, May 4, 1954, fewer than 300 were still alive.

Each night he told his men, "We must hold one more day. The Americans will not let us down...they may come."

The ground shook under Corporal Antoine Hoinant as a shell hit. Dirt and steel clanged down on his helmet. He did not believe that the Americans would come. Officers were telling their men that a rescue army was fighting to break through the enemy ringed around Dien Bien Phu. The rescue army would save them.

Liars!

Hoinant could remember back six months ago to when his paratrooper battalion had flown here to Dien Bien Phu (pronounced De-yen Be-yen Foo). They had been ordered to capture this valley in North Vietnam. "You will find no Vietnamese troops at Dien Bien Phu," officers told Hoinant and his buddies. Minutes later they leaped from their low-flying planes.

Vietnamese machine-gunners sprayed the paratroopers as they floated down into the dark-green valley. When the paratroopers hit the ground, Vietnamese soldiers leaped on them, stabbing chests and slitting throats. But after a day of bloody hand-to-hand fighting, the French paratroopers captured Dien Bien Phu. They were soon reinforced by more troops, including Major Bigeard's paratroopers.

French troops had been fighting in what they called French Indochina for almost two centuries. In the early 1800s the French conquered Vietnam and neighboring Cam-

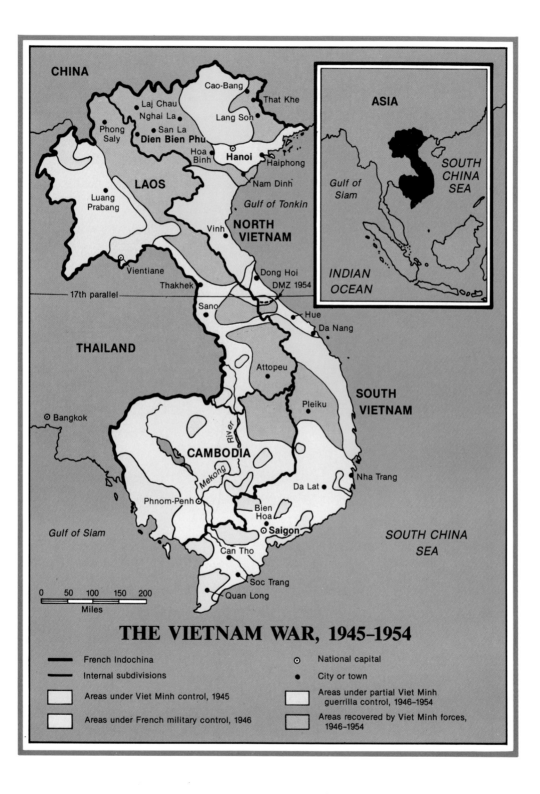

THE VIETNAM WAR, 1945-1954

CHINA

Cao-Bang
That Khe
Laj Chau
Nghai La
Lang Son
Phong
Saly
San La
Dien Bien Phù
Hoa
Binh
Hanoi
Haiphong
LAOS
Nam Dinh
Gulf of Tonkin
Luang
Prabang
Vinh
NORTH
VIETNAM
Vientiane
Thakhek
Dong Hoi
DMZ 1954
17th parallel
Sano
Hue
Da Nang
THAILAND
Attopeu
Pleiku
SOUTH
VIETNAM
Bangkok
River
Mekong
CAMBODIA
Nha Trang
Da Lat
Phnom-Penh
Bien
Hoa
Saigon
SOUTH CHINA
SEA
Gulf of Siam
Can Tho
Soc Trang
Quan Long

ASIA

Gulf of
Siam

SOUTH
CHINA
SEA

INDIAN
OCEAN

0   50   100   150   200
Miles

▬ French Indochina	⊙ National capital
— Internal subdivisions	• City or town
☐ Areas under Viet Minh control, 1945	☐ Areas under partial Viet Minh guerrilla control, 1946–1954
☐ Areas under French military control, 1946	☐ Areas recovered by Viet Minh forces, 1946–1954

bodia and Laos (see map on page 9). Vietnam became a French colony just as India was conquered by the British and made a British colony. French and English settlers were given land in the colonies. They hired peasants at cheap wages. The settlers became rich sending fruit, vegetables, tin, oil, and rubber back to the home country.

In 1940, early in World War II, Germany's Adolf Hitler conquered France. Hitler's ally, Japan, grabbed French Indochina and most of the other European colonies in Southeast Asia. After Japan's defeat in 1945, the victorious United Nations powers, including the United States, gave Indochina back to the French.

But native leaders rose all across Southeast Asia and demanded that the European settlers leave. "Give our land back to our people!" shouted Vietnamese leaders, such as the bearded, willowy Ho Chi Minh. Ho Chi Minh organized a rebel army and began to fight what he called a "war of national liberation." He compared himself to George Washington leading a rebel army to throw the British colonists out of America.

On September 2, 1945, Ho Chi Minh proclaimed the independence of Vietnam from French rule. For seven years, Ho Chi Minh's rebels had fought French tanks and planes with homemade grenades and hunting rifles. When the French roared into Vietnamese villages with their tanks and big guns, Ho Chi Minh's guerrillas vanished like ghosts

As a teenager, the Vietnamese leader Ho Chi Minh was jailed
by the French for demanding that his country be liberated
from France. By 1941, he had organized the Vietminh,
a political party dedicated to Vietnamese independence.

into the jungle. At night the jungle fighters sneaked out to ambush and kill the French as they slept.

United States President Dwight Eisenhower feared that Communist Russia and China would take over such Asian countries as Vietnam, Laos, and Cambodia, making leaders like Ho Chi Minh their puppets. The United States and the Soviet Union were glowering angrily at each other in what was called the cold war. No shots were fired, no bombs dropped. But Russia's ruler, Joseph Stalin, feared that America wanted to destroy his Communist system. America's leaders feared Stalin wanted to spread communism around the globe—starting in Southeast Asia.

In 1953, the United States began to send guns, tanks, and planes to the French to wipe out Ho Chi Minh's rebels. Ho Chi Minh turned to Russia and China for weapons.

Late in 1953, French generals decided to lure Ho Chi Minh into a battle they were sure they would win. The French captured Dien Bien Phu, figuring that Ho Chi Minh would try to retake the valley. Ho Chi Minh needed a crossroads at Dien Bien Phu to get supplies to his troops. By early 1954, more than 14,000 French soldiers held Dien Bien Phu. The French hoped Ho Chi Minh would throw his troops into an all-out fight for the valley. In a slugging match, the French figured, they could easily wipe out the rebels with their bombers, guns, and tanks. Ho's jungle fighters had neither bombers nor tanks.

But Ho did have thousands of peasants willing to strain

their arms and backs. The peasants hauled 200 huge guns, called "Iron Elephants," by the Vietnamese, up steep jungle trails, and over mountains. Inch by inch, pulling the cannons as slowly as a half mile (.8 km) a day, the peasants tugged the Iron Elephants more than 200 miles (320 km) to Dien Bien Phu. Vietnamese soldiers hid the guns in caves above Dien Bien Phu. From the valley the French could not see the guns.

Then, one terror-filled night, March 12, 1954, the 200 guns roared. Shells whined down on the French. More than 500 Frenchmen died on one hill, their bodies tossed about like rag dolls. On another hill some 700 men ran, screaming, toward the valley. Exploding shells shook them off their feet. Flying fragments tore off legs and arms. Fewer than 200 bloody survivors stumbled into trenches. One survivor gasped, "It was a massacre."

The massacre had dragged on for two months. Pinned down in the valley, French soldiers saw comrades blown away as Vietnamese guns raked their trenches. Bombs shattered the French landing strip, leaving huge craters. No troops could be flown to the Dien Bien Phu garrison. Nor could the wounded be airlifted to hospitals.

Bruno Bigeard's paratroopers drank muddy water from streams filled with dead men. Paratroopers died of fever. Doctors ran out of medicine.

One woman tried to help the wounded. She was army nurse Genevieve de Galard-Terraube. She moistened the dry lips of men screaming with pain. She whispered prayers with the dying. The soldiers called her "the Angel of Dien Bien Phu."

On the morning of May 7, 1954, fewer than 8,000 French soldiers still stood. More than 3,000 were dead; another 3,000 lay dying or too sick or injured to fight.

American generals urged President Eisenhower to save the French by dropping small atomic, or A-, bombs on the Vietnamese ringing Dien Bien Phu. Eisenhower said no. The Russians, he feared, might hurl A-bombs at the French, setting off a nuclear war that would destroy the world.

Near noon on May 7, Corporal Hoinant heard shouts from outposts across the valley: "Here they come…here they come.…"

Ho Chi Minh's rebels swarmed over the exhausted, stunned, and sick French, shouting, "Hands up! Surrender!" An hour later Major Bigeard and Corporal Hoinant stood in long lines with 8,000 other French prisoners. The Vietnamese marched them to prison camps. Fewer than half— Bigeard, Hoinant, and nurse Galard-Terraube among them— would live to go back to France.

Two months later, the French and the Americans sat down with Ho Chi Minh and delegates from China in Geneva, Switzerland. They signed an agreement. It was agreed that (1) Vietnam would be divided until 1956 into North Vietnam and South Vietnam, and (2) in 1956 free elections would decide who would rule a united Vietnam. Ho Chi

Minh took control of North Vietnam, establishing his capital at Hanoi. A Vietnamese general, the tiny 4-foot-9-inch (1.45-m) Ngo Dinh Diem, took control of South Vietnam, with his capital at Saigon.

But the elections would never take place. Bullets—not ballots—would decide the future of a place more than 2 million American soldiers would soon call Nam.

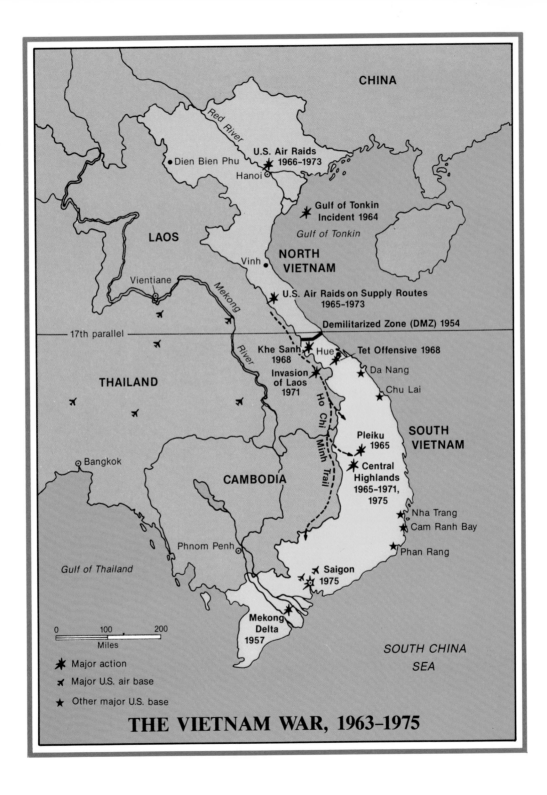

THE VIETNAM WAR, 1963-1975

THE GREEN BERETS

AN AMERICAN GI, Sergeant Steve Kornie, watched the black-clad North Vietnamese guerrillas trot across the mushy rice field. Within minutes they would charge this South Vietnamese fort, their Russian AK-47 assault rifles blazing. South Vietnamese soldiers bunched behind Sergeant Kornie in the midnight darkness. He told them to hold their fire until Ho Chi Minh's jungle fighters came within a few yards of the fort.

The blond, lanky Kornie knew he was surrounded. He guessed the North Vietnamese guerrillas outnumbered his South Vietnamese soldiers by three to one.

Almost ten years had gone by since the battle of Dien Bien Phu, and it was now the summer of 1963. No elections had been held to unite North and South Vietnam under one government. Two American presidents—Eisenhower from 1956 to 1960, then John Kennedy—worried that Ho Chi Minh, an idol to many Vietnamese, would win the election and take over the new nation. Kennedy agreed with Eisenhower, who felt that if the Communists won Vietnam, dozens of other countries in Asia would topple and fall under the Communist heel.

The United States sent planes, tanks, and guns to South Vietnamese president Ngo Dinh Diem. Kennedy ordered some 15,000 American soldiers, called "Special Forces" troops, to go to Vietnam to teach Diem's Army of the Republic of Vietnam (ARVN) how to fight Ho's guerrillas. Sergeant Kornie was one of those Special Forces soldiers. They wore round green caps and called themselves the Green Berets.

The first North Vietnamese shells exploded near the bunkers of ARVN soldiers, most of them between seventeen and eighteen years of age. Broken, bleeding bodies crashed against sandbags. A machine gun chattered from a nearby bunker, mowing down wide-eyed ARVN soldiers.

"What's gone wrong?" shouted another Green Beret to Kornie. That bunker had been held by the ARVN.

"The VC! They're on that bunker!" Kornie shouted.

The VC were the Viet Cong, Ho Chi Minh's guerrilla fighters in South Vietnam. Kornie saw dozens of black-uniformed VC scurrying like ants over more bunkers held by the South Vietnamese.

Kornie spun around and reached for a black box. Wires snaked out of the box. The wires connected handles in the box to a dozen explosive land mines he had planted in the bunkers. Kornie yanked one of the handles.

President John F. Kennedy tells reporters how "Communist rebels" were poised to invade South Vietnam.

Sheets of blue-and-orange flame shot from the bunkers. Black bodies twirled high into the suddenly bright sky. Blood spattered the sandbags piled in front of Kornie.

Waves of shrieking VC stormed at Kornie and his ARVN soldiers, whose guns spit red-and-white fire.

Kornie was suddenly flying backward. He crashed into a wall. He saw flames and smoke fanning across the front of his bunker. An enemy shell had just missed a direct hit that would have blown Kornie and his soldiers to bits.

Kornie rose groggily to his feet. The Green Berets had been told not to fight the VC, only to train ARVN soldiers, since America was not at war. "We've got to get out of here!" he shouted to the other Green Berets.

They clambered up a nearby bunker. In the darkness they heard a bugle. The Green Berets knew the bugler was signaling a new charge by "Charlie," as they called the VCs.

"Make a run for it," an ARVN officer told Kornie. "We'll cover for you."

Blood streamed down the face of the officer. "Thanks," Kornie said, gripping the officer's hand.

A sudden, snarling roar made both look upward. In the light of exploding shells, they saw two American T-28 fighters zoom low over the battlefield. Their .50-caliber machine guns sprayed bullets among the scattering Viet Cong. The planes dropped napalm bombs. The bombs exploded, throwing tongues of white-hot flame that turned men into human torches.

Left: President Kennedy sent the Green Berets to train South Vietnamese soldiers to be jungle fighters and to "win the hearts and minds of the Vietnamese people."

Below: South Vietnamese (ARVN) soldiers often came from small villages. The sons of peasants, they had little military training before going into combat.

Helicopters carried American and South Vietnamese
troops into remote jungle areas to fight the Viet Cong.
Helicopters were also used as gunships to strafe the
enemy and as flying ambulances to rescue the wounded.

Sergeant Kornie led ARVN soldiers as they chased the fleeing Charlies, streaming bullets into their backs. Kornie stumbled over corpses charred by napalm.

With American guns, tanks, and bombers, the ARVN blasted the Viet Cong out of hundreds of villages in South Vietnam. But when the Green Berets and the ARVN left to fight elsewhere, the VC crept back to the villages. They terrorized or killed village chiefs. The VC forced the villagers to feed and house the Cong's soldiers.

In Saigon, the capital of South Vietnam, Buddhist priests burned themselves alive in the streets. They were protesting General Diem's dictatorship, which had closed their temples. Diem's killers murdered anyone who called for free elections. He jailed political foes, charging they were Communists.

By the fall of 1963, Kennedy knew he was losing what he called "the battle for the hearts and minds of the Vietnamese people." He decided Diem had to be overthrown. In November, South Vietnamese generals murdered Diem.

A group of generals, led by a 6-foot (1.8-m) General Duong Van ("Big") Minh, took over as South Vietnam's rulers. Three weeks later another president was murdered – Kennedy. By 1964, his successor, Lyndon B. Johnson, had come to believe that only a massive blow by America's military strength could win the war and save South Vietnam and Asia from communism.

Ho Chi Minh's Viet Cong and his regular North Vietnam-

Villagers flee from the fighting in South Vietnam.
Many feared they would be killed by the Viet Cong if they
refused to give the guerillas food and hiding places.

South Vietnamese soldiers hunt for Ho Chi Minh's guerrillas on a "search and destroy" mission. Those missions burned villages and killed civilians, angering peasants caught between the Viet Cong and the ARVN.

ese troops now occupied three-fourths of South Vietnam. The ARVN and Green Berets held only the big cities and towns. They went out on "search and destroy" missions to kill the Viet Cong. South Vietnamese peasants worked in rice fields during the day, then slipped on VC uniforms at night. They hated the ARVN and Green Berets, who destroyed their villages and killed women and children while searching for Charlies.

In Washington, President Johnson looked for a way to squash the Viet Cong with hundreds of thousands of American soldiers, tanks, and bombers. He would find that way in the choppy, foggy waters of a bay called Tonkin.

THREE

ROLLING THUNDER

COLONEL LARRY GUARINO dipped the nose of the plane. His F-105 Thunderchief flashed down at his target—a bridge in North Vietnam. Puffs of smoke billowed around the cockpit as antiaircraft gunners on the ground whizzed shells at the diving fighter-bomber. The Thunderchief suddenly shook violently. A shell had thumped into the Thunderchief's belly. The shock tossed Guarino so hard his hands flew off the controls. Guarino gasped, choking, as the cockpit filled with smoke. He grabbed the ejection handles, blowing open the top of his cockpit. Moments later he twirled upward, ejected from the stricken plane.

He heard a loud pop. His parachute had opened. He floated down into North Vietnamese territory. Another F-105 circled above him to mark where he landed. Guarino knew a rescue helicopter was already clattering across the sky to pluck him to safety.

Guarino's Thunderchief was one of hundreds of American planes dropping bombs on the North Vietnamese in North and South Vietnam. As part of an attack code-named Rolling Thunder, the U.S. Air Force was hailing bombs on the Ho Chi Minh Trail. The trail snaked through jungles for hundreds of miles from North to South Vietnam. Ho Chi Minh's soldiers came down the trail carrying weapons for the Viet Cong guerrilla fighters who were now swarming all over South Vietnam.

In the summer of 1964, President Johnson had found the way to throw a heavyweight punch at Ho Chi Minh. Cruising in fog off North Vietnam in the Gulf of Tonkin, two American warships reported being attacked by North Vietnamese torpedo boats. The warships later reported not being sure if the underwater torpedoes had actually been fired at them. But President Johnson obtained authority from Congress it was called the Gulf of Tonkin Resolution, to send American troops and ships to attack Ho Chi Minh's guerrillas. "We must defend ourselves," Johnson told Congress.

By the summer of 1965, more than 60,000 American fliers, soldiers, and sailors had poured into Vietnam to fight

An aerial view of an American convoy of troops and supplies snaking through the jungles of South Vietnam—or what American GIs called "the boondocks."

Above: Vice President Lyndon B. Johnson (front row, second from left) poses with American and foreign officials during a visit to Saigon in 1961. Johnson feared that if the United States lost Vietnam to communism, the Democrats would be blamed and be voted out of the White House.

Left: American soldiers stream into Vietnam, with more than half a million of them arriving from 1965 to 1967.

side by side with the South Vietnamese army. In turn, the Soviet Union and China supplied Ho Chi Minh with modern weapons.

A Russian ack-ack gun had just knocked Colonel Guarino's plane out of the sky. Landing near a jungle, he threw off his chute and radioed his position to an F-105 pilot circling above. Guarino's radio crackled: "Help is on the way, Larry."

The husky, dark-haired Guarino panted up a steep, muddy hill. At the top he could be seen by the rescue helicopter. He slipped, skidding into a stream. He looked up into the mouth of a rifle, gripped by a North Vietnamese soldier.

Other soldiers knotted a rope around Guarino's arms. They led him to a hut in the jungle. Guarino heard the rescue chopper roar low, searching for him on the hill. It hovered 20 feet (6 m) from the hut. But Guarino had to sit still, the gun inches from his head. The copter flew off.

That night Guarino sat in a dirty, smelly prison cell, his ankles chained. The soldiers took him to Hanoi, the North Vietnamese capital. Thrown into a cramped cell, he was beaten and tortured along with hundreds of other American prisoners of war.

Meanwhile, American marines and soldiers—who called themselves grunts—crept through jungles and splashed across rice fields to root out Viet Cong strongholds. The grunts walked warily, their eyes searching the ground. Plastic mines hid under leaves. One step on the wrong leaf

Above: South Vietnamese soldiers stand over captured Viet Cong guerrillas. Prisoners on both sides were often tortured by the enemy for information, then shot.

Left: American officers study maps and charts before sending out patrols on seek-and-destroy missions.

would blow off a man's legs. At night the grunts slept in slimy holes, attacked by snakes, rats, and by crawling creatures that could kill with one bite.

For a week Roy Scott's Second Infantry Battalion, 327th Regiment, had been searching for Charlie in the Truong Luong Valley. So far the lanky Scott and his buddies had killed more than one hundred Cong. Twelve Americans had been killed or wounded. Near dusk one evening, the grunts dug foxholes on a hill overlooking the valley.

Scott glanced at his watch. It was 0530, military time for 5:30 in the morning. Dawn's first light streaked across the crimson horizon. Scott heard the mooing of cows, then the whistle of an incoming shell.

The blast threw Scott against a tree, breaking his arm in three places. He ran to a machine gun and began to fire with his good hand.

Bullets zipped over the helmets of Americans who stood up in their holes. "They're coming up behind the cows!" someone shouted. American guns chattered and roared. The grunts heard the terrified bellowing of animals amid the howls of the charging Cong.

Sergeant Charles Proctor crept to the brow of the steep hill. He saw Viet Cong climbing upward, crouched low. Head down, Proctor pulled the firing pin from a grenade and rolled it down the slope.

The grenade exploded, tearing in half a Charlie only 10

feet (3 m) away. Proctor peered over the hill and saw a half dozen mangled bodies tumbling down the slope.

At the bottom, the Cong crouched behind the bodies of the cows. They dropped shells into the cigarlike barrels of their mortars. The shells whistled into the American foxholes on the hill. Proctor dived into a hole. He shouted to his men: "Throw all the grenades you got!"

The grunts hurled the baseball-size grenades down the slope. But they had to throw blindly, keeping low in their foxholes as hunks of razor-sharp metal whizzed above them. The hill looked as though on fire, with smoke and flames licking into the air.

Proctor heard the stuttering roar of a Russian AK-47 assault rifle no more than a few feet away. The Cong raced across the top of the hill. They sprayed slugs into grunts caught in their holes. Wounded men screamed and shouted for medical help: "Medic...over here...medic...."

A deafening clatter filled the air overhead. Proctor looked up from his hole and saw a huge American helicopter, called a gunship. Its nose gunners whizzed rockets that blew away Charlies as they fled down the slope.

Proctor scrambled out of his hole. Bodies littered the hill, the grass a purplish red. Looking down the hill, he saw Viet Cong staggering into the jungle, vanishing in the thick foliage.

Proctor counted twenty dead Cong. Six Americans had been killed, a dozen wounded.

American and ARVN soldiers clamber into a boat to cross
a river in South Vietnam. Some grunts (American marines
and soldiers) befriended the South Vietnamese; others looked
down upon them, calling them racial slurs, like "gooks."

Back home in America that night, families watched TV news shows. Vietnam was called the "Living Room War." For the first time, Americans were getting a daily look at the horrors of war. They saw Americans streaming bullets into straw houses in Vietnamese villages. They heard newscasters give the latest body count of dead Cong. American generals were claiming as many as 2,000 VCs killed in a single day.

By 1967, almost 500,000 Americans were fighting in Vietnam. More than 16,000 Americans had been killed, almost 100,000 wounded. Armless and legless Nam veterans hobbled down American streets. Some Americans, called doves, demanded that President Johnson pull out of Vietnam. They argued that Americans were fighting for a military dictatorship. Generals like "Big" Minh still ruled South Vietnam.

But other Americans, called hawks, argued that America should step up the war against North Vietnam, even blowing the country to bits with atomic bombs. If the United States lost in Vietnam, they argued, communism would spread like a plague across Asia. Millions of Asiatic Communists, some said, could one day overwhelm America.

Many young doves, including college students, refused to be drafted into the army. They burned their draft cards on street corners and campuses. Thousands fled to Canada or Europe. Millions of students marched on campuses demand-

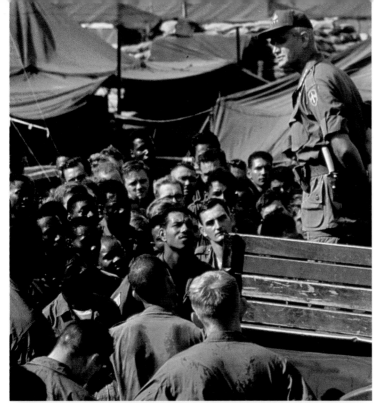

General William Westmoreland (in the truck), the United States's commanding general in Vietnam, gives a pep talk to his troops, telling them what they were fighting for in Vietnam. But many American soldiers never understood what the war was all about.

South Vietnamese soldiers, many of them not even twenty years old, listen to a briefing on why they are fighting. Most were poorly paid, earning wages the equivalent of less than a dime a day.

ing that President Johnson end the war. They chanted, "Hey, hey, LBJ, how many men did you kill today?"

Some Americans had begun to ask: "If we are killing thousands of VCs a month, how can Ho Chi Minh keep on fighting much longer?"

Ho Chi Minh would soon give them an answer.

FOUR

TET

THE SIX Vietnamese men shouted holiday greetings to other people celebrating on a crowded street in Saigon. Suddenly, the men ducked into a dark alley, glancing over their shoulders. They shrugged off their jackets and pulled on the inky-black uniforms of the Viet Cong. From bags they yanked out rifles, grenades, and submachine guns.

They could hear the shouts of people singing as they came home from parties. The time was 1:30 in the morning, January 30, 1968, the Vietnamese New Year's Day.

North and South Vietnam had called a truce for Tet, the Vietnamese name for the New Year. But thousands of Viet Cong, wearing civilian clothes, had sneaked into Saigon and dozens of other cities in South Vietnam.

The Viet Cong soldiers jumped into a waiting taxicab. Minutes later the cab jerked to a stop in front of the gates of the American headquarters in Saigon. Two marine sentries stood guard at the embassy, where the United States ambassador to South Vietnam was sleeping. A Viet Cong leaped from the cab, his AK-47 automatic rifle whizzing slugs. The marines ducked behind gates and sounded an alarm.

An explosion rocked the darkness, streaked now with red and white lines of tracer bullets. Cong bombs blew a hole in the wall around the headquarters. A wave of VCs flooded through the hole. They pumped bullets and rocket-grenades at pajama-clad marines firing rifles from windows.

Ho Chi Minh's Tet offensive had begun. Viet Cong soldiers raced through streets in other South Vietnam cities. They slaughtered American and South Vietnamese soldiers still sleepy after parties. The VC captured Hue, a major city. They set up antiaircraft guns to blast at American bombers. American pilots bombed the homes of people they had come 10,000 miles (16,000 km) to save from communism. Hundreds of men, women, and children fell bleeding, wounded or dead, as grunts and ARVNs shot at the Cong in streets and houses.

Meanwhile, 10,000 U.S. marines fought for their lives in hills near a place north of Saigon called Khe Sanh. North Vietnamese troops ringed Khe Sanh, pouring down fire and death on the Americans. "This is another Dien Bien Phu," American reporters cabled back to the United States.

Haggard marines huddled in trenches. Rats bit their arms, legs, and faces whenever they tried to sleep. Marines held hands to their ears as American B-52 bombers dropped tons

The streets and buildings of Hue were ravaged during the days of street fighting between ARVN troops and VCs. After the Tet onslaught, President Johnson's chief military adviser, Clark Clifford, recommended that Americans withdraw from Vietnam.

of bombs on North Vietnamese soldiers dug into holes less than a football field away. Marine corporal James Hebron told Americans what life was like at Khe Sanh for more than a month:

"All you saw was the air being ripped apart and the ground shaking underneath you — and you bouncing into the air... the trenches would shake...."

The marines held at Khe Sanh. The Americans and ARVN hurled the Cong out of the cities. More than 4,200 Americans and ARVN were killed, another 16,000 wounded, maimed, or blinded. But Ho Chi Minh suffered about 45,000 dead and 100,000 wounded. Ho Chi Minh lost the Tet offensive — but he had made a huge step toward winning the war.

Tet made President Johnson and many Americans doubt for the first time that America could squash Ho Chi Minh. Almost every minute of each day, the body of a dead American was coming home from Vietnam for burial. In 1968, the war-weary president decided not to run for reelection. He asked the North Vietnamese to sit down for peace talks.

The talks began in Paris. But all sides — the Americans, the North Vietnamese, and the South Vietnamese — could

American marines wait in their trenches during a lull in the fighting at Khe Sanh. In the midst of the seventy-seven-day Khe Sanh battle, President Johnson ordered his aides to make a study of whether the war could ever be won. He left office before the study was finished.

As in every war, people on both sides mourned their dead. *Right:* Standing on Vietnamese soil, a peasant woman grieves at the grave of a war victim.

Below: An American serviceman and woman carry the remains of a dead American, listed previously as Missing in Action, to a plane in Hanoi that would then fly the remains back to the United States for burial.

A dead American soldier is carted away
from the fighting by his buddies. A battered
U.S. flag is in the foreground.

Americans gather in
Washington, D.C., to protest
an increasingly unpopular war.
By 1970, younger people were
more likely to be doves;
older people and blue-collar
workers tended to be hawks.

not even agree on where to sit at the conference table. Americans would learn that no peace would come from these and future talks; peace would only come after victory on the battlefield.

By now about 2 million American men and women had served in Vietnam. More than 40,000 had died and another 260,000 were wounded. Some came home mentally damaged and became drug addicts.

In 1969, the new president, Richard Nixon, said he would demand that the South Vietnamese take over most of the fighting. Then, he said, the Americans now in Vietnam—almost 550,000—could go home. But one American diplomat in South Vietnam said that "99 percent of the Vietnamese people hoped that the war would go away and leave them alone."

Meanwhile, millions of Americans marched for peace in Washington and other cities and on campuses. "Bring the troops home!" they shouted. Others sang, "Give peace a chance!" But many other Americans called them traitors. "There can be no peace without victory," they shouted back at the peace marchers.

Vietnam had drawn the American people wider apart than at any time since the country had been split by slavery and the Civil War a hundred years earlier. Like that civil war, the Vietnamese war would now spill blood on American soil.

FIVE

PEACE

ON THIS WARM and hazy spring day in May 1970, nineteen-year-old Allison Krause joined hundreds of other students in a march for peace. They chanted the antiwar slogan "One, two, three, four, we don't want to go to war," as she and her friends walked up a grassy slope on the Kent State University campus in Ohio. They faced troops armed with rifles, the muzzles aimed straight at the peace marchers.

Ohio officials had sent National Guard troops to Kent State after someone set fire to a building. Seeing the troops, students hurled stones at the helmeted soldiers.

Soldiers heard an order to fire. Dozens of rifle shots cracked in the still air. Students screamed and ran. One toppled, blood streaming down his face. A second fell, then a third. A bullet struck Allison Krause in the head. Within minutes she and three other students were dead, eleven others wounded.

Shocked Americans saw on the next day's front pages a photograph of a young woman kneeling over one of the fallen students, horror in her eyes. The Kent State killings swung many Americans over to the side of the doves.

By now the Paris peace talks had stopped. Ho Chi Minh had died in 1969. North Vietnam's new leaders said they would agree to peace talks only if there were elections that would unite North and South Vietnam under one government. The South's ruling generals claimed that North Vietnam would win the election by cheating.

President Nixon told Americans that the South Vietnamese could win the war by themselves with American guns and planes. He promised to shrink the size of the American forces in Vietnam. But he worried that the bigger North Vietnam Army would overwhelm the South's ARVN. The ARVN was also shrinking as weary soldiers deserted by the thousands.

Nixon tried to help the ARVN. He knew that the North Vietnamese had built bases in neutral Cambodia. Their soldiers slipped into Vietnam to ambush ARVN soldiers. Then they ran back to Cambodia, whose boundaries the ARVN could not cross. Nixon ordered American and ARVN troops to invade Cambodia and destroy the bases. He also gave secret orders for American bombers to blow up those bases.

"Nixon is widening the war, not ending it as he had promised," protested many Americans. Others read with

A camouflaged South Vietnamese soldier grips
an automatic weapon at a place where the
North Vietnamese were creeping into South Vietnam.

horror and rage of Americans slaughtering Vietnamese women and babies in a village called My Lai. The American soldiers had killed the villagers because they thought the villagers were aiding the Viet Cong. Congress told Nixon: "No more money for the Vietnam War."

Nixon's secretary of state, Henry Kissinger, met in Paris with the North Vietnamese. Early in 1973 they signed a cease-fire agreement. The United States agreed to take its troops and planes out of Vietnam. An election would be watched over by neutral nations. The election would decide who ruled Vietnam.

The North Vietnamese released Colonel Guarino and thousands of other prisoners of war. Colonel Guarino came home to be greeted by a son who had been in high school when he was captured. That son had since graduated from college and flown as a fighter pilot over the Hanoi prison that held his father.

No cheering crowds greeted the returning veterans of Vietnam. They marched in no victory parades. They saw anger, even hate, in the eyes of neighbors. Some people accused them of being like the baby killers at My Lai. Many Americans had become embarrassed by Vietnam's defeats and cruelties. They wanted to forget the men who had fought there.

The North and South Vietnam leaders soon were bickering again. They could not agree on how to guarantee an honest election. Meanwhile, some Americans feared that the North Vietnamese still held Americans as prisoners of war

(POWs). Thousands of Americans were listed as missing in action (MIAs), their bodies never found. Were those MIAs, people asked, actually being held as prisoners? Those Americans wanted no peace in Vietnam until the North Vietnamese accounted for every American.

North Vietnamese troops drove deeper into South Vietnam. Congress refused to send any more weapons to the ARVN as it reeled backward toward Saigon.

On April 30, 1975, the North Vietnam Army smashed into Saigon. The ARVN troops held up their hands in surrender.

North Vietnamese tanks rumbled toward the United States headquarters. A few hundred marines and civilians gathered on the roof. Helicopters droned down to pluck them off the roof and carry them to waiting warships.

Thousands of South Vietnamese men, women, and children jammed the streets around the headquarters. They had worked for the Americans. Weeping, they pleaded to be taken away on the helicopters.

But there was no more space on the crowded helicopters. The pro-American Vietnamese were left behind. Many were jailed, tortured, or killed by the North Vietnamese.

The Vietnam War became the first war that the United States lost. More than 58,000 American men and women were killed, another 365,000 wounded. Many of the wounded were maimed, paralyzed, or blinded for life. At least a million and a half Vietnamese soldiers and civilians had died.

What do Vietnam veterans tell their children and grandchildren about that war? Many, like Connecticut veteran

Above: North Vietnamese troops celebrate the "liberation" of Saigon as an armored tank rolls into the city.

Facing page: When Saigon fell to the North Vietnamese, thousands of frantic South Vietnamese men, women, and children fought to get aboard helicopters and transport carriers bound for the United States.

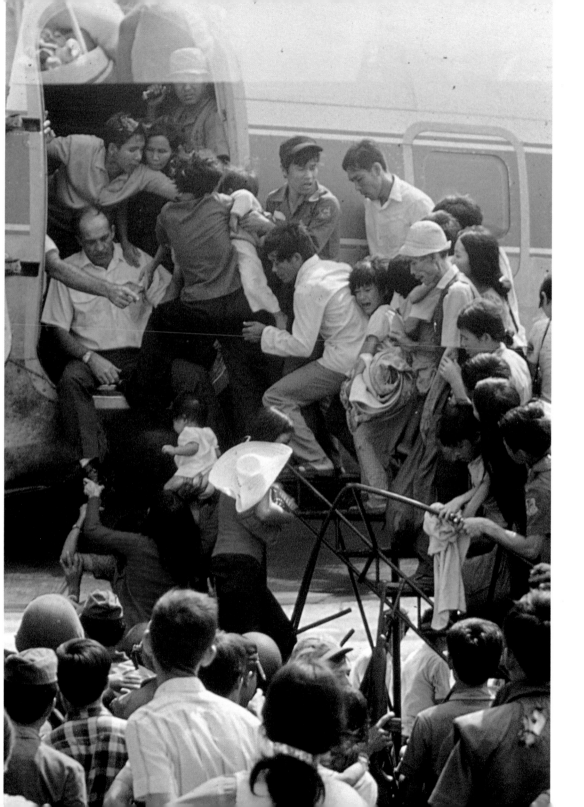

The Vietnam Veterans Memorial in Washington is an
eternal tribute to those men and women—their names are
engraved on the wall—who lost their lives in Vietnam.

William Lane, say that movies and television do not show what the war was really like.

"The men I knew in Vietnam," Lane says, "weren't on drugs. We didn't murder civilians. We didn't hate the war or LBJ or our country."

"Some of the bravest and best men that ever wore an American uniform," he adds, "fought in that war. They deserve better," he says, than to be shown in movies "as a legion of losers."

Others tell of their anger at being ignored or insulted when they came home. Says a former grunt, Tim O'Brien: "When I was wounded in Vietnam, my blood ran just as heavily and my pain was just as strong as my father's . . . in other wars."

Some can never forget the killing of civilians. "I was like a hired gun," says Lou Carello from his wheelchair. "I still can't sleep without a light on." He has nightmares that the people he killed "are going to get me."

Like many war veterans, most hoped that their war would be the last war. One Nam veteran, Dave Christian, tells of seeing a dead Cong soldier with a cross around his neck. "He believed in God and I believed in the same God. And I thought . . . we are brothers in the same world and we are killing each other. . . ."

Many others agree with a Bardstown, Kentucky, veteran who said when asked why he went to Vietnam: "I love this country, and my country asked me to go. And that's the reason why I went—willingly."

IMPORTANT DATES ABOUT THE WAR IN VIETNAM

1946   Ho Chi Minh's Vietnamese rebels begin attacks on French forces who had reoccupied French Indochina in 1945 after the Japanese surrender that ended World War II. Ho's Vietminh organization declares Vietnam an independent state.

1954   The Vietminh defeat the French in the Battle of Dien Bien Phu, and the French agree to sign peace agreements in Geneva, Switzerland. Vietnam is divided at the 17th parallel into North and South Vietnam. The Geneva agreement calls for elections in 1956 to unify the country under one ruler.

1955   General Ngo Dinh Diem wipes out opponents and becomes president of South Vietnam. He argues that the Communist government of North Vietnam, ruled by Ho Chi Minh, would not allow a fair election in 1956. The elections are not held. Ho Chi Minh argues that South Vietnam has broken the Geneva agreement.

1957 Members of Ho's Vietminh organization, living in South Vietnam, start a rebellion to overthrow Diem. The rebels are called Viet Cong (Vietnamese Communists) by Diem, although not all of the rebels believe in communism. To stop the spread of Russian Communist power in Southeast Asia, President Eisenhower sends weapons and advisers to Diem's ARVN (Army of the Republic of Vietnam). Communist China and the Soviet Union send arms to Ho, who sends them to the Viet Cong fighting Diem in the south.

1961–1963 The Viet Cong rebels grow in size and seem ready to topple Diem. President Kennedy rushes 15,000 American Green Beret soldiers to train the ARVN in jungle warfare.

1963 A Buddhist priest burns himself alive to protest Diem's dictatorship. ARVN generals murder Diem early in November and install General Nguyen Khanh as president of South Vietnam. On November 22, President Kennedy is assassinated.

1964 Two U.S. warships report being attacked off North Vietnam in the Gulf of Tonkin. Congress passes the Gulf of Tonkin Resolution approving "all necessary measures" to prevent more attacks. President Johnson sees the resolution as approval for all-out war against the Viet Cong and North Vietnam.

1965 U.S. marines land in Vietnam early in March and go into action against the Cong at Pleiku – the first major battle between Americans and the Cong.

1968 On Tet, the Vietnamese New Year, the Cong sneak into South Vietnamese cities, including Saigon, where they attack the U.S. embassy building. They capture one city. They suffer more than 100,000 casualties but prove to many Americans back home that America's armed might cannot snuff them out.

1969 President Nixon announces the beginning of the withdrawal of American troops from Vietnam.

1970 Nixon orders an invasion of neutral Cambodia, where North Vietnamese troops have built bases. He also orders bombings of Laos and Cambodia. Growing antiwar protests by Americans make Nixon decide to end the invasion and the bombings.

1973 Late in January the United States, North Vietnam, and South Vietnam sign a peace agreement. The United States agrees to take its soldiers out of Vietnam. Fighting soon resumes between the North and South Vietnamese.

1975 North Vietnamese troops enter Saigon, which is re-named Ho Chi Minh City, as the ARVN surrenders. A few hundred American marines are hurriedly airlifted by heli-copters. The United States has spent an estimated $500 billion on a war in which it dropped more bombs on Vietnam than it had dropped on Europe during World War II. Some Americans believe that American men still languish in North Vietnam as prisoners of war.

FOR FURTHER READING

Edwards, Richard. *The Vietnam War.* Vero Beach, Fla.: Rourke Enterprises, 1986.

Lawson, Don. *An Album of the Vietnam War.* New York: Franklin Watts, 1986.

Lawson, Don. *The War in Vietnam.* New York: Franklin Watts, 1981.

Maclear, Michael. *The Ten Thousand Day War.* New York: St. Martin's Press, 1981.

Moore, Robin. *The Green Berets.* New York: Crown Publishers, 1965.

INDEX

Page numbers in *italics* refer to illustrations.

ABOUT THE AUTHOR

JOHN DEVANEY is the author of more than thirty books for young adults. His most recent books include a five-book series on World War II. The first three books cover the years 1941 (*America Goes to War*), 1942 (*America Fights the Tide*), and 1943 (*America Turns the Tide*). Mr. Devaney teaches writing at Fordham University. He and his wife, Barbara, an art director, live in Mahattan. They have two sons, John and Luke.